You Are What You Eat

Date: _____

Yummy ID Card

My name is _____ .
My surname is _____ .
I'm _____ years old.
I'm _____ tall.

Paste your photo here

My favourite food is _____
I like _____ and _____
but I don't like _____
I really hate _____
I'm allergic to _____

I enjoy (tick ✓):
☐ cooking
☐ doing experiments
☐ learning new things
☐ eating

My fingerprint

Cook for Fun - Level A   © Copyright ELI 2006   Worksheet 1.1

You Are What You Eat

Date: _____

Food Pyramid Puzzle

You need:

cardboard 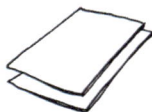 glue    scissors  felt-tip pens   magazines

This is a famous
P _ _ _ _ _ _ _

Instructions:

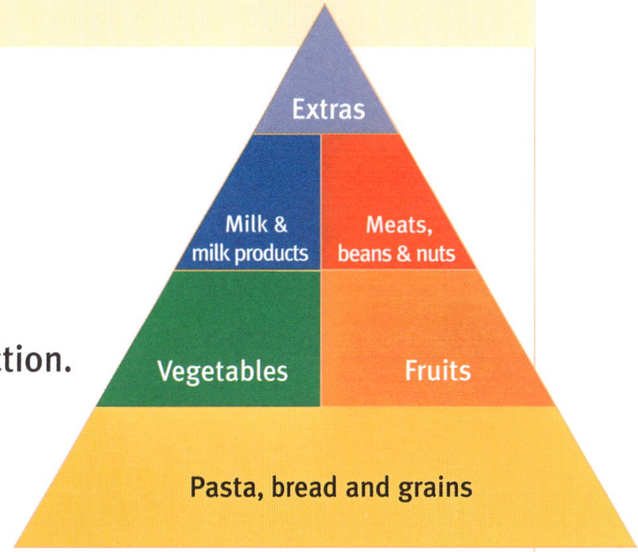

1. Draw a big pyramid.
2. Divide it into 6 sections.
3. Colour each section a different colour.
4. Write each food group in the right section.
5. Cut out each section.
6. Cut out lots of different foods from magazines.
7. Paste the food on the pyramid.
8. Rearrange the pyramid.

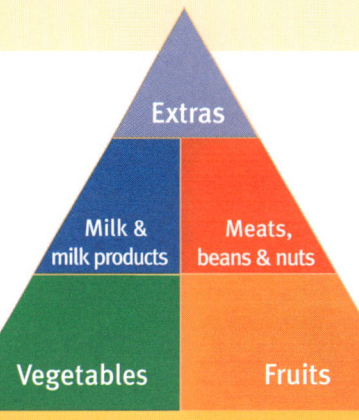

Cook for Fun - Level A   © Copyright ELI 2006   FACT FILE 2   Worksheet 1.2

You Are What You Eat   Date: _____

Getting Ready: Are Your Hands Clean?

✏️ Draw. You need:

cooking oil	cinnamon	sink	soap	a teaspoon and a tablespoon

Rub 1 tablespoon of cooking oil all over your hands.   Sprinkle 1 teaspoon of cinnamon on your hands.

Wash hands for 20 seconds 🕐

Student 1: wash hands with cold water and no soap.

Student 2: wash hands with warm water and no soap.

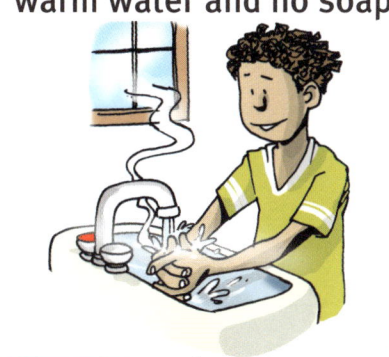

Student 3: wash hands with warm water and soap.

Draw hands after washing.

☐ dirty ☐ quite clean ☐ very clean

Draw hands after washing.

☐ dirty ☐ quite clean ☐ very clean

Draw hands after washing.

☐ dirty ☐ quite clean ☐ very clean

Cook for Fun - Level A   © Copyright ELI 2006   Worksheet 1.3

Pumpkin

Date: _____

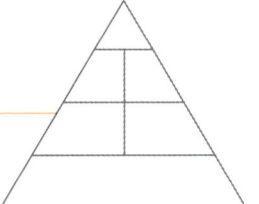

Recipe — **Pumpkin Pie**

Complete with the keywords: flour , eggs , milk , pumpkin , pie , brown .

1 cup of mashed _____   1 cup of _____ sugar   1/2 cup of _____

  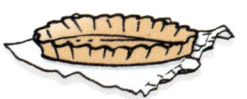

2 _____   1 tablespoon of _____   1 _____ shell

Instructions:

Step one: Mix pumpkin, sugar, milk and egg yolks.

yolk

Step two: Pour into pie shell.

Step three: Bake at 240°C for 35 minutes.

Put some whipped cream on your pie!

Report
☐ Good
☐ Ok
☐ Yucky

Cook for Fun - Level A   © Copyright ELI 2006   Worksheet 2.1

Pumpkin

Date: _____

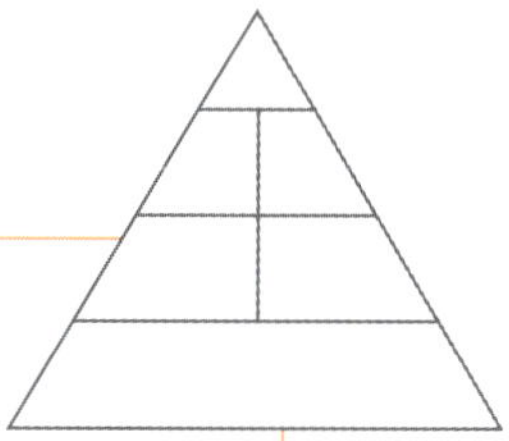

Halloween Pumpkin Mask

Complete with the keywords: paper (2) , scissors , orange , tape , stick , ten minutes , brush , pencil .

Make your Halloween Pumpkin Mask!

A  _____ plate

B  _____ paint

C  Black _____

D  _____k

E   B_____

F  Sticky ____p__

G   S_____

H  T____ m_____

I  P_____

Instructions:

1. Paint your plate with orange paint.
   You need: A B E

2. Let it dry for ten minutes.
   You need:

3. Draw the nose and the mouth on the black paper.
   You need:

4. Cut out eyes, nose and mouth.
   You need:

5. Fix the stick with sticky tape.
   You need:

Wear your Halloween pumpkin mask!

BOO!

Cook for Fun - Level A © Copyright ELI 2006 Worksheet 2.2

Pumpkin

Date: _____

Pumpkin Is Good for You

Match and fill in the blanks.

Pumpkin contains:

FIBRE	VITAMIN A	POTASSIUM
It is good for our intestines.	It is good for our eyes and for our hair.	It is good for our muscles!

  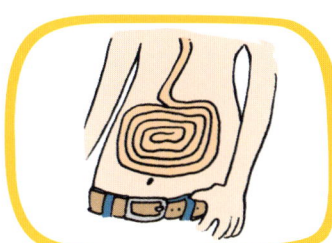

E _ _ _ and H _ _ _   M _ _ _ _ _ _ _   I _ _ _ _ _ _ _ _ _ _

Colour the orange fruit and vegetables.

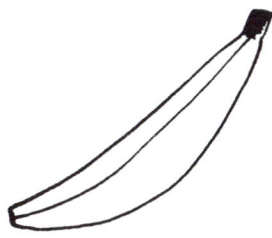  

Banana   Apricot   Lettuce

  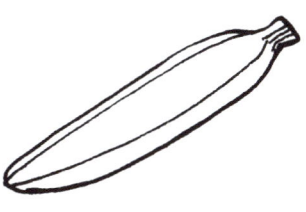

Carrot   Melon   Courgette

My favourite orange fruit/vegetable is ....

Cook for Fun - Level A   © Copyright ELI 2006   Worksheet 2.3

Dairy Products   Date: _____

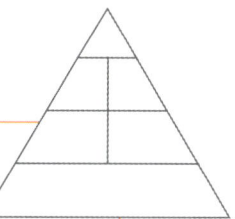

The Milk Group

Complete the sentences:

Milk group foods help your _____S and _____TH.

Milk group foods come from C_____'s _____K.

bones	cow	milk	teeth
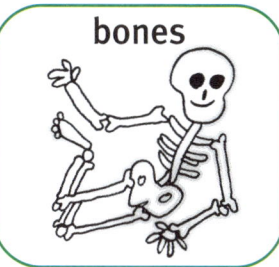			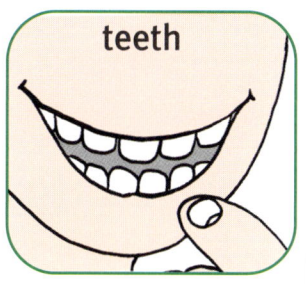

Milk group foods include ... Tick (√):

milk	hamburgers	fish	cheese	tomatoes

☐ yes	☐ yes	☐ yes	☐ yes	☐ yes
☐ no	☐ no	☐ no	☐ no	☐ no

Can you think of other foods in the milk group? ✏️ Draw and 🖊 write.

Foods in the milk group contain ... (✏️ Circle).

Proteins   *Coffee*

Glue

Calcium   *Fat*

Cook for Fun - Level A   © Copyright ELI 2006   Worksheet 3.1

Dairy Products

Date: _____

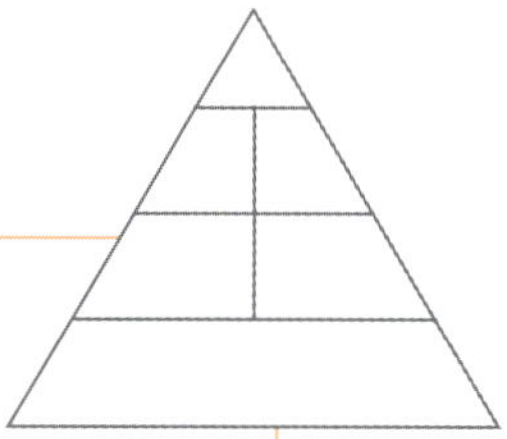

🎧 A Rhyme — Little Miss Muffet

Little Miss Muffet
Sat on a tuffet,

Eating her curds and whey.

Then came a big spider,
That sat down beside her,

And frightened
Miss Muffet away.

She's eating C _ _ _ _ and _ H _ _

Recipe

You need:
- 2 cups of milk
- 3 tablespoons of vinegar
- salt
- a stove

1 Warm milk and vinegar in a saucepan.

2 Stir 5 to 8 minutes.

3 Remove the saucepan from the heat. Stir.

4 Strain the curds.

5 Add salt. Eat with fruit or bread.

Curds are:
- ☐ cheese
- ☐ glue
- ☐ fish

Report
- ☐ Good
- ☐ Ok
- ☐ Yucky

Cook for Fun - Level A   © Copyright ELI 2006   Worksheet 3.2

Dairy Products

Date: _____

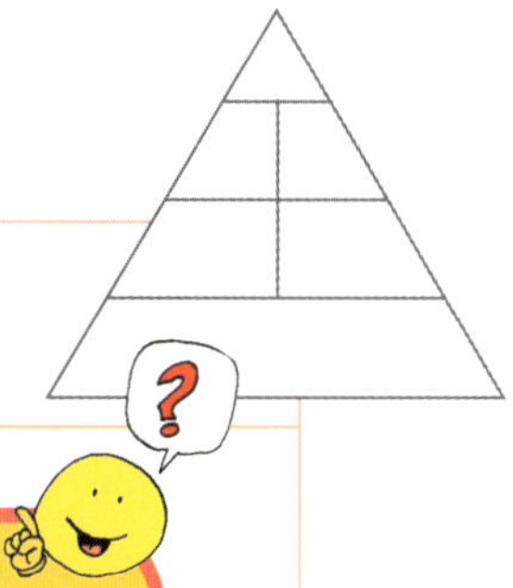

Recipe

Homemade Butter

Let's make butter!

Butter comes from:
☐ cream ☐ oil ☐ eggs

you need:

cream

a glass jar with a lid

1 Put the cream in the jar.

2 Close with the lid.

3 Shake, shake, shake and shake!

4 Take it in turns. It can take a long time.

The butter is ready!

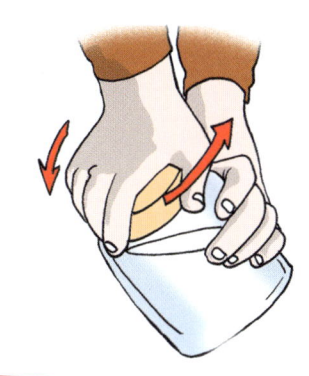

Eat your butter on bread. Sprinkle with sugar or salt.

Report

With sugar	With salt
☐ Good	☐ Good
☐ Ok	☐ Ok
☐ Yucky	☐ Yucky

Colour the areas of the tongue where you taste sugar or salt.

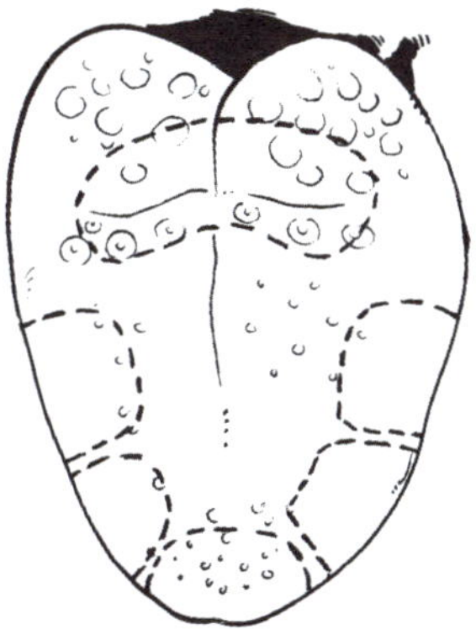

Cook for Fun - Level A   © Copyright ELI 2006   FACT FILE 4   Worksheet 3.3

Yogurt

Date: _____

Yogurt Is Alive!

What is yogurt?

It's M _ _ K  with "friendly bacteria" in it.

Friendly bacteria protect your I _ _ _ _ _ _ _ _ S

Yogurt is rich in ...
- ☐ proteins
- ☐ calcium
- ☐ potassium

Recipe: Let's make yogurt!

✏️ Draw.

you need:
warm milk (30/40°)
yogurt culture
a jar

| milk | yogurt culture | jar |

1 Put the milk and the yogurt culture in the jar and stir.

2 Leave in a warm place for 24 hours.

3 What can you see?

4 Strain the yogurt.

5 Eat or put it in the fridge.

6 Use the culture to make more yogurt.

It is delicious with fruit or honey!

Report
- ☐ Good
- ☐ Ok
- ☐ Yucky

Cook for Fun - Level A   © Copyright ELI 2006

Worksheet 4.1

Yogurt

Date: _____

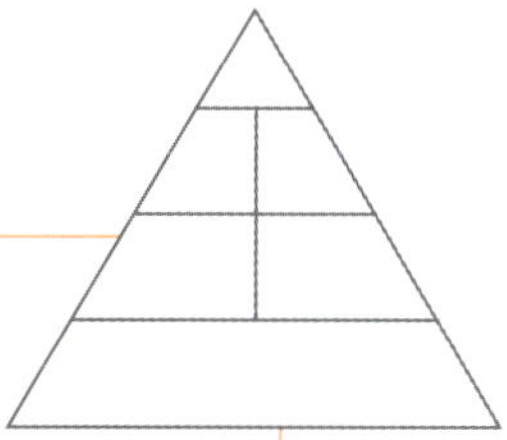

A Recipe

Tzatziki

✏️ Colour Greece on the map.

Tzatziki is a Greek starter.

Ingredients:

6-8 cloves of garlic

500 g of full fat Greek yogurt

1 tablespoon of olive oil

1 tablespoon of vinegar

1 cucumber

salt

1 Crush the garlic in a garlic press.

2 Mix the garlic with the yogurt in a bowl.

3 Add oil, vinegar and salt.

4 Wash the cucumber.

5 Peel and slice the cucumber.

6 Put the cucumber in the bowl with the yogurt.

7 Eat with warm "pita bread".

Report
☐ Good
☐ Ok
☐ Yucky

Cook for Fun - Level A © Copyright ELI 2006

Worksheet 4.2

Yogurt

Date: _____

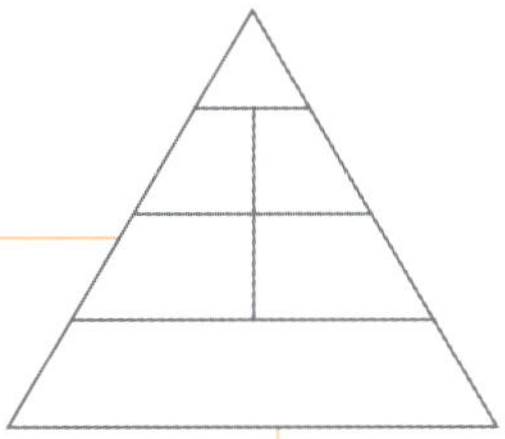

Beauty Recipes

Yogurt Walnut Scrub

Ingredients

1/4 cup of plain yogurt

1/4 cup of walnuts (very finely ground)

 Mix ingredients together.

 Wet your face then gently rub into your skin.

 Rinse off with warm water.

Orange Yogurt Mask

Ingredients

1 tbsp. of plain yogurt

the juice of 1/4 of an orange

 Mix ingredients together.

 Leave on your face for five minutes.

 Rinse off with warm water.

Which is your favourite mask? Tick (v) and ✏ write a slogan.

My favourite mask is
....

Because it's:

- refreshing ☐
- healthy ☐
- relaxing ☐
- energizing ☐
- other ....

Cook for Fun - Level A   © Copyright ELI 2006

Worksheet 4.3

Christmas Food

Date: _____

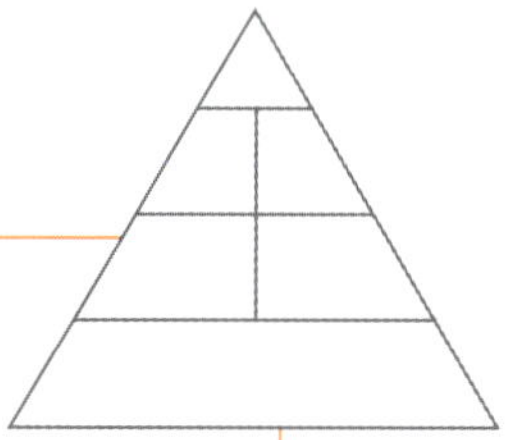

🎧 A Rhyme — Little Jack Horner

Find the rhyme and fill in the blanks. Use the keywords: plum , pie , corner .

Little Jack Horner
Sat in the _____ ,

Eating a Christmas _____ :

He put in his thumb,
And pulled out a _____ ,

And said, "What a good boy am I!"

Look at your food pyramid and ✎ colour the circles.

Recipe — Christmas Pie

Ingredients:

Pie shell:
- ○ 12 tbsp. flour
- ○ 4 tbsp. sugar
- ○ 1/2 cup of butter

Filling:
- ○ 1/2 cup of brown sugar
- ○ 1/3 cup of flour
- ○ 1/2 tsp. of cinnamon
- ○ 3 cups of plums
- ○ 1 tbsp. of lemon juice
- ○ 1 tbsp. of margarine

Cook for Fun - Level A   © Copyright ELI 2006   Worksheet 5.1

Christmas Food   Date: _____

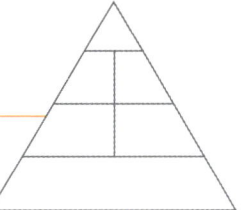

Food at Christmas

Circle the correct season and complete.

CHRISTMAS is on December 25th. CHRISTMAS is in ...

Spring   Summer   Autumn   Winter

In .... it is very **COLD**. When it's cold we need **ENERGY!**

Some food gives little energy. Some food gives a lot of energy.

Little   Some   A lot of

Food Quiz   What food gives a lot of ENERGY?

A lot of energy = ✓
Little energy = ✗

 nuts	☐	 butter	☐
 carrots	☐	 bread	☐
 chocolate	☐	 cookies	☐
 cakes and pies	☐	 water	☐
 lettuce	☐	 tomatoes	☐

Count the correct answers: ☐

Cook for Fun - Level A   © Copyright ELI 2006   Worksheet 5.2

Christmas Food   Date: _____

Christmas in the World

Complete with the keywords: beach , bread , Japanese , trees , biscuits , torrone .

Greece

Christopsomo ("Christ's Bread") is a decorated _____ .

India

Children decorate banana _____ for Christmas.

Egypt

A traditional Christmas dish is *Ghryba*. They are _____ .

Spain

A traditional Christmas treat is *turron*, similar to Italian '_____' .

 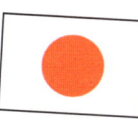
Japan

A popular _____ decoration for peace and joy is the swan.

Australia

People have their Christmas party on the _____ !

✎ Write.

Christmas in my country.

My favourite Christmas decoration is ....

I eat ....

A traditional dish is ....

I celebrate with ....
....

Cook for Fun - Level A   © Copyright ELI 2006   Worksheet 5.3

Ginger

Date: _____

Ginger ID

Zingiber Officinale

This is Ginger.

Write its scientific name:

....

....

Origin: China

Medical properties: it is good for your stomach. It helps digestion.

This is the FL ___ R

This is the P_A__

This is the R_O_

We use the powder from the root for cooking. **Smell it!**

It smells   good ○   ok ○   yucky ○

It smells like   bananas ○   chocolate ○   lemons ○

Game Smell and guess.

What is it?

 Onion ○

 Lemons ○

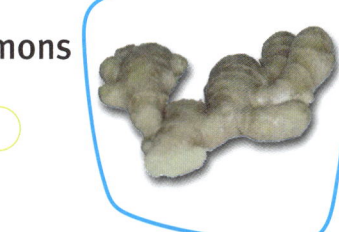 Ginger ○

 Apple ○

 Garlic ○

 Cheese ○

Cook for Fun - Level A   © Copyright ELI 2006   Worksheet 6.1

Ginger

Date: _____

🎧 A Story The Gingerbread Man

Fill in the gaps. Use the keywords: river , dog , cow , woman , man , fox .

An old _____ makes a Gingerbread Man.

She puts him in the oven.

She opens the oven door.
The Gingerbread Man runs away.

The Gingerbread Man meets a _____

The Gingerbread Man meets a _____

The Gingerbread Man comes to a _____

A _____ says "I can help you!"
The fox opens his mouth … and 'Snap!'

That was the end of the Gingerbread _____!

Ginger

Date: _____

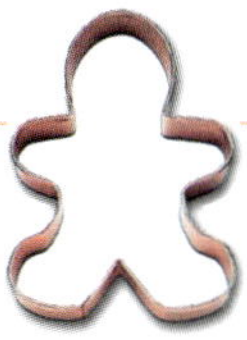

Recipe: The Gingerbread Man

Match the pictures with the names of the ingredients.

INGREDIENTS:

- 3 cups of flour
- 1/4 tsp. of salt
- 1 tbsp. of ginger
- 12 tbsp. of butter
- 1 1/2 cups of brown sugar
- 1 egg
- 1 tbsp. of vanilla
- 1 tbsp. of baking soda

Fill in the gaps. Keywords: ten , sugar , ingredients , butter .

| Mix dry _____. | Mix butter and brown _____. Add the egg. | Stir dry ingredients into the _____ mixture. Add vanilla. |

| Roll it. | Cut it. | Bake seven to _____ minutes at 350°. |

Report
- [ ] Good
- [ ] Ok
- [ ] Yucky

Cook for Fun - Level A © Copyright ELI 2006 Worksheet 6.3

Fruit

Date: _____

5 a Day

We contain vitamins and minerals

We are beautiful

Yummy!

Fruit and vegetables: look good, taste great and contain vitamins and minerals. Your body needs 5 servings a day!

Fill in the gaps and match.

Vitamin A is good for your E_____ and H_____.

Vitamin C protects you from C_____.

Vitamin is very good for your N_____ and S_____.

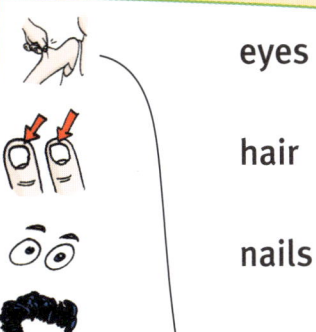

- eyes
- hair
- nails
- colds
- skin

Write your favourite fruit or veggies for each colour.

....

....

ALWAYS wash fresh fruit and vegetables.

Cook for Fun - Level A   © Copyright ELI 2006

Worksheet 7.1

Fruit

Date: _____

Preserving Fruit

Fruit and vegetables can be:

FRESH 	FROZEN 	CANNED 	DRIED 

Drying is a natural method of preserving fruit. Let's try!

✎ Draw.

Choose some fruit.	Wash and slice the fruit.	Dry the fruit in the sun for four days.

✎ Draw and tick (✓).

Dried fruit	Fresh fruit	Which one do you prefer?
		☐ dried ☐ fresh
		☐ dried ☐ fresh
		☐ dried ☐ fresh
		☐ dried ☐ fresh
		☐ dried ☐ fresh

Cook for Fun - Level A   © Copyright ELI 2006

Worksheet 7.2

Fruit

Date: _____

Fruit from the World

✏️ Draw the fruit, 🖊 write the name, match it to its country.

- Coconut
- Pineapple
- Dates

Cook for Fun - Level A   © Copyright ELI 2006

Worksheet 7.3

Fruit

Date: _____

Arcimboldo's Fruity Faces

This is a famous painting by Giuseppe Arcimboldi.

✏️ Write. How many fruits and vegetables can you see?

....
....
....
....
....
....
....
....

Now it's your turn!

1 Cut up your fruit.

2 Make a funny picture on your plate.

3 Eat it!

Cook for Fun - Level A   © Copyright ELI 2006

Worksheet 7.4

Seeds and Nuts

Date: _____

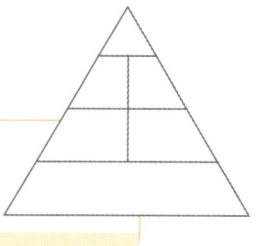

Sunflower Seeds

✏️ Draw a sunflower and tick (✓):

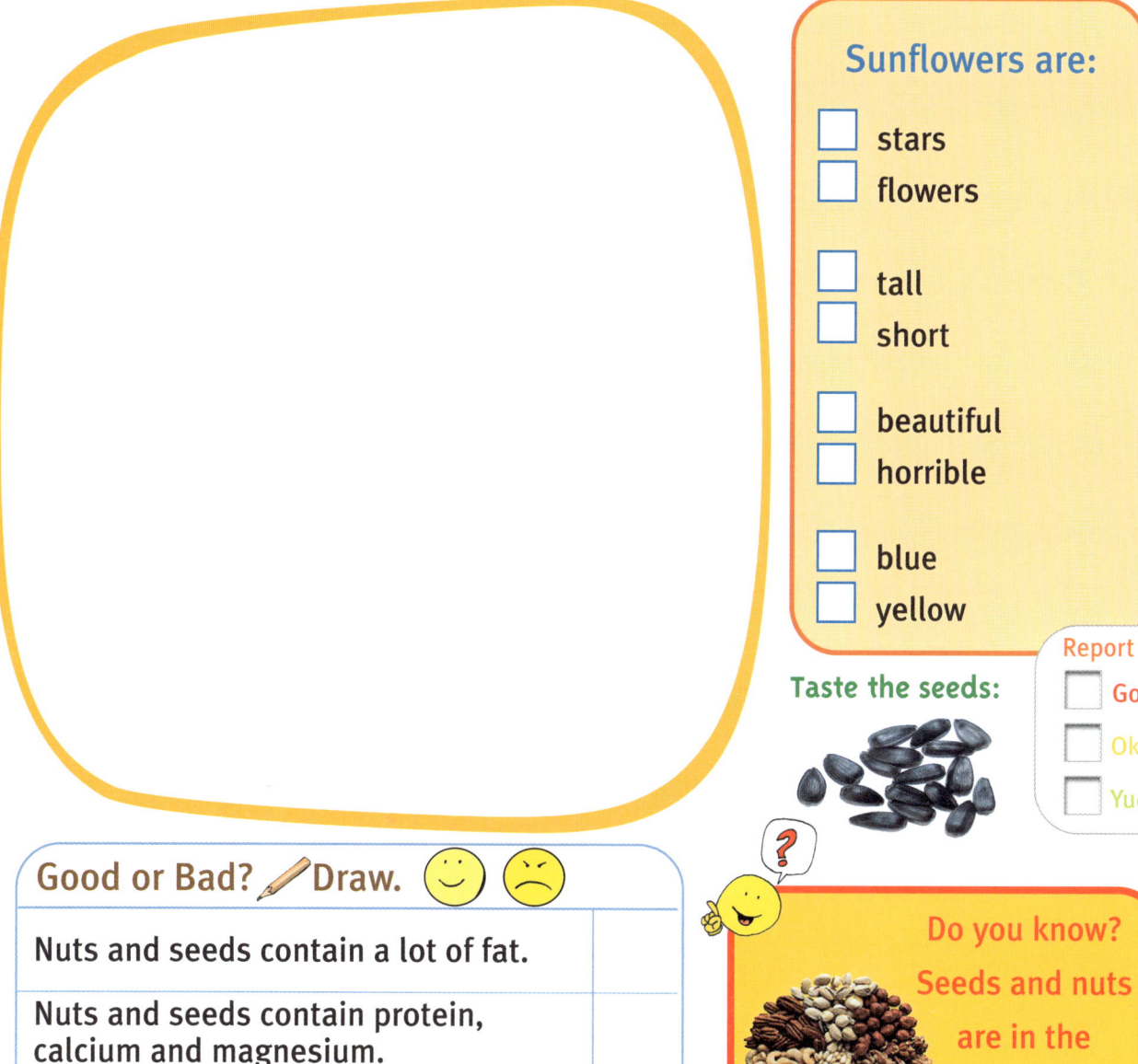

Sunflowers are:

- ☐ stars
- ☐ flowers

- ☐ tall
- ☐ short

- ☐ beautiful
- ☐ horrible

- ☐ blue
- ☐ yellow

Taste the seeds:

Report
- ☐ Good
- ☐ Ok
- ☐ Yucky

Do you know? Seeds and nuts are in the .... group.

Good or Bad? ✏️ Draw. 😊 ☹️

Nuts and seeds contain a lot of fat.	
Nuts and seeds contain protein, calcium and magnesium.	
Nuts and seeds contain no cholesterol.	
Nuts and seeds are high in calories.	

✏️ Circle the best option:

Don't eat nuts and seeds.

Eat in moderation.

Eat lots of nuts and seeds.

Cook for Fun - Level A © Copyright ELI 2006   FACT FILE 2   Worksheet 8.1

Seeds and Nuts

Date: _____

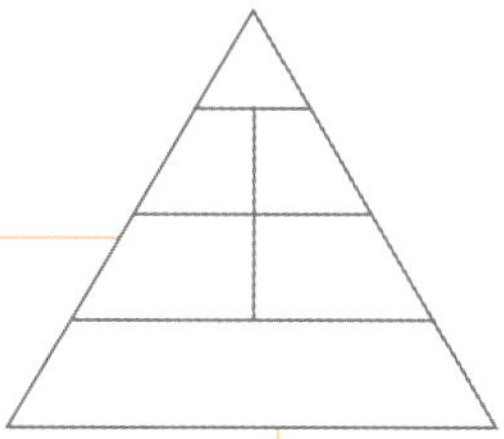

Sprouting Seeds

You can grow seed sprouts from:

- [ ] alfalfa
- [ ] clover
- [ ] sunflower
- [ ] lentils 
- [ ] peas
- [ ] soya beans
- [ ] wheat 
- [ ] rice
- [ ] spelt

Follow the instructions.

You need:
- jar
- water
- (alfalfa) seeds
- mesh
- rubber band

Soak 2-3 tablespoons of alfalfa overnight.

Close the jar with the mesh and the rubber band. Strain water.

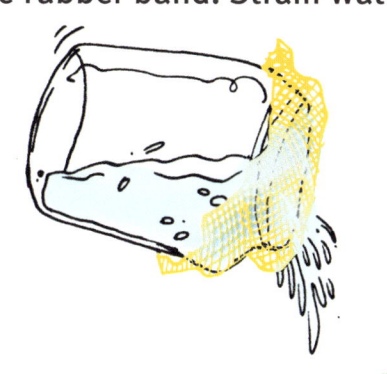

Wait for your seeds to sprout.

Make your cheese and seed sprout sandwich.

EAT YOUR SANDWICH!

Report
- [ ] Good
- [ ] Ok
- [ ] Yucky

Make a cress head

INSTRUCTIONS
Dampen cotton wool. Put cress seeds in a yogurt pot or in an egg carton. Wait!

Make a cress caterpillar

Cook for Fun - Level A © Copyright ELI 2006

Worksheet 8.2

Bread

Date: _____

Experiment: Yeast in Action!

Yeast makes bread rise. Look at the bubbles in a slice of bread.

Baking powder is a kind of yeast.

✏️ Draw. You need:

baking powder	1 cup of warm water	2 tbsp. of sugar	a large rubber balloon	a small empty water bottle

Use the keywords: water , sugar , bottle , balloon , baking powder .

1 Put the _____ _____ and the _____ in the cup of warm _____ and stir.

2 Pour the mixture into the _____ .

3 Attach the _____ to the mouth of the bottle.

4 ✏️ Draw what you see.

Cook for Fun - Level A   © Copyright ELI 2006

Worksheet 9.1

Bread

Date: _____

A Story — Lord Sandwich

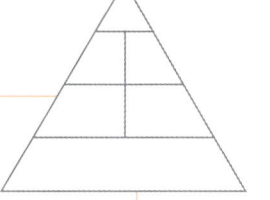

Listen and mime.

Panel 1: England, 1762. "Hello, my name is Lord Sandwich."

Panel 2: "I love playing card games."

Panel 3: "It's time for dinner, sir."

Panel 4: "I don't have time for dinner: I'm playing! Put my dinner between two slices of bread."

Panel 5: (in the kitchen)

Panel 6: "Oh, that's a sandwich!"

Cook for Fun - Level A © Copyright ELI 2006

Worksheet 9.2

Bread

Date: _____

Sandwich Competition

Cut outs: create your sandwich. ✏️ Write.

Face = 2 slices of bread

Eyebrows =
....
....

Eyes =
....
....

Mouth =
....
....

Nose =
....

Hair =
....

My sandwich!

✏️ Draw.

✏️ Write the ingredients.

Ingredients

Report
- ☐ Good
- ☐ Ok
- ☐ Yucky

Cook for Fun - Level A   © Copyright ELI 2006   Worksheet 9.3

Fish

Date: _____

At the Fish Market

What can you buy? Tick (v) and write.

clams	shrimps	scallop
☐ yes ☐ no Price €_____	☐ yes ☐ no Price €_____	☐ yes ☐ no Price €_____
salmon	**mussels**	**crab**
☐ yes ☐ no Price €_____	☐ yes ☐ no Price €_____	☐ yes ☐ no Price €_____
trout	**sardines**	**lobster**
☐ yes ☐ no Price €_____	☐ yes ☐ no Price €_____	☐ yes ☐ no Price €_____
prawns	**oyster**	**sole**
☐ yes ☐ no Price €_____	☐ yes ☐ no Price €_____	☐ yes ☐ no Price €_____

Cook for Fun - Level A   © Copyright ELI 2006

Worksheet 10.1

Fish

Date: _____

Fish is Good for You!

Match.

Fish is good for... your brain

Fish contains proteins, vitamins, minerals and healthy oils. Eat fish 3 times a week!

your heart

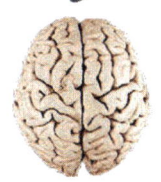

your body

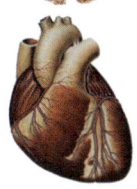

Taste and guess. Do you like it?

tuna	anchovies	smoked salmon	sardines
☐ yes ☐ no	☐ yes ☐ no	☐ yes ☐ no	☐ yes ☐ no

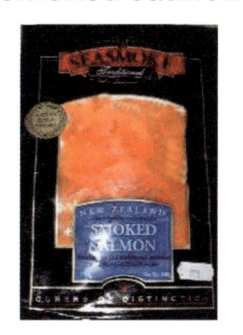

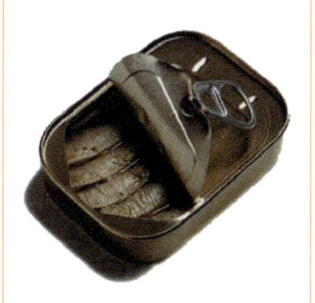

My favourite fish salad:

Ingredients:

Dress with:

salt ☐
pepper ☐
vinegar ☐
lemon ☐
olive oil ☐

Cook for Fun - Level A   © Copyright ELI 2006

Worksheet 10.2

CookForFun – Cut Outs

Worksheet 6.2

Menu

Starters

Main Course

Desserts

Drinks

Worksheet 9.3

CookForFun - Mind Map

My Favourite Activities

- You Are What You Eat
- Pumpkin
- Dairy Products
- Yogurt
- Christmas Food
- Ginger
- Fruit
- Seeds and Nuts
- Bread
- Fish

Cook for Fun

Nutrition Education

CookForFun A - Index

Topics	Worksheets
1 You Are What You Eat	1.1 Yummy ID Card 1.2 Food Pyramid Puzzle 1.3 Getting Ready: Are Your Hands Clean?
2 Pumpkin	2.1 A Recipe: Pumpkin Pie 2.2 Halloween Pumpkin Mask 2.3 Pumpkin Is Good for You
3 Dairy Product	3.1 The Milk Group 3.2 A Rhyme: Little Miss Muffet 3.3 A Recipe: Homemade Butter
4 Yogurt	4.1 Yogurt Is Alive! 4.2 A Recipe: Tzatziki 4.3 Beauty Recipes
5 Christmas Food	5.1 A Rhyme: Little Jack Horner 5.2 Food at Christmas 5.3 Christmas in the World
6 Ginger	6.1 Ginger ID 6.2 A Story: The Gingerbread Man 6.3 A Recipe: The Gingerbread Man
7 Fruit	7.1 5 a Day 7.2 Preserving Fruit 7.3 Fruit from the World 7.4 Arcimboldo's Fruity Faces
8 Seeds and Nuts	8.1 Sunflower Seeds 8.2 Sprouting Seeds
9 Bread	9.1 Experiment: Yeast in Action! 9.2 Lord Sandwich 9.3 Sandwich Competition
10 Fish	10.1 At the Fish Market 10.2 Fish is Good for You

Cut-outs   Mind Map   Certificate

© 2007 – ELI s.r.l.
P.O. Box 6 – 62019 Recanati – Italy
Tel.: +39 071 750701 - Fax: +39 071 977851
www.elionline.com – e-mail: info@elionline.com

HandsOnLanguage
Cook for Fun A
by Damiana Covre and Melanie Segal

Graphic design by Studio Cornell sas
Illustrated by Roberto Battistini

This book is sold subject to the condition that it shall not, by way of trade or otherwise, be lent, resold, hired out, or otherwise circulated without the publisher's prior consent in any form of binding or cover other than that in which it is published and without a similar condition including this condition being imposed on the subsequent purchaser.

Printed in Italy by Tecnostampa – 06.83.235.0

ISBN 10	88-536-1031-X	Cook for Fun - Worksheet A
ISBN 13	9788853610317	
ISBN 10	88-536-1032-8	Cook for Fun - Worksheet B
ISBN 13	9788853610324	
ISBN 10	88-536-1033-6	Cook for Fun - Special Guide + Audio CD
ISBN 13	9788853610331	

Cook for Fun
Nutrition Education in English

Level A

Certificate

This is to certify that

....

has completed
a Cook for Fun Project
with excellence

Date ....   Teacher(s).........................

HandsOnLanguage
Cook for Fun A
by Damiana Covre and Melanie Segal

© 2007 – ELI s.r.l.
P.O. Box 6 – 62019 Recanati – Italy
Tel.: +39 071 750701 – Fax: +39 071 977851
www.elionline.com
e-mail: info@elionline.com